OVER LONDON

OVER LONDON

A CENTURY OF CHANGE

JASON HAWKES
WITH AEROFILMS

TEXT BY IAN HARRISON

HarperCollins*Illustrated*

CONTENTS

INTRODUCTION

In 1921, when the earliest of the photographs in this book was taken, George V was on the throne, David Lloyd George was Prime Minister, and Queen Elizabeth II had not even been born. Although 1921 may not sound a long time ago, momentous changes have occurred in the intervening years. In that year, police patrols in London began using motorcycles for the first time, unemployment in Britain topped a million, and Hitler was voted President of the German Nazi Party; while a miners' strike ended with the government agreeing to subsidize the price of coal, and Sinn Fein prisoners were released, following the signing of an Anglo-Irish Treaty. Some things change; others don't.

In France in the same year, the first helicopter made its shaky maiden flight amidst great excitement, hitting international headlines. Almost eighty years later, booking a helicopter to take the colour pictures for this book was a matter of routine for photographer Jason Hawkes, who had to dodge between the air ambulance, the 'flying eye' and air traffic in and out of London City Airport. It was a far cry from the biplanes, with their wire stays for strengthening the wings, used for Aerofilms' early photography. Jason Hawkes had been inspired by the unique insight these old photographs give into London's past, and decided to re-create the same views, providing graphic evidence of how much the city has changed. The result is a book that combines the fascination of the aerial photograph with the fun of 'spot the difference'.

There is something about an aerial photograph that invites closer and more detailed inspection than a conventional view: people who wouldn't look twice at an ordinary picture of a bridge, street or railway station will stare long and hard at an aerial photograph, imagining themselves in the picture and comparing the perspective with the view at ground level. Aerial views give a sense of power – the power to see around corners, through buildings, over obstacles, and to see the connections between places that are never apparent on the ground. *Over London* goes a step further: by juxtaposing old and new pictures, the book provides a unique look back through time.

In some photographs, where nearly everything has changed, the little that does remain the same becomes significant. Often dwarfed by more recent buildings or hidden from view by a new development, the older buildings give a heightened perspective to what has altered. The appearance of a new building in the City is not in itself surprising, but the sight of a church spire from the older picture peeping out from behind it tells another story: not only does it connect the new building with what has gone before it, but it is a reminder that we are not at the end of the story, that the new building is just another episode in an ongoing tale. In other pictures where little has altered, there is satisfaction in noticing even the smallest of changes – a new house on the corner of a street, an extension in a back garden, trees planted or cut down.

Each chapter looks at a different part of London, each with its own flavour. First, the City, the country's financial heart, where the symbolic bowler hat has been usurped by the slick designer suit; then, the West End, where cinemas and glitzy restaurants have replaced the music halls and oyster houses; third, the East End and Docklands, where the most sweeping social and physical changes have taken place; and last, a look further afield at the many and varied residential areas of North, West and South London. Together, these comparisons provide a portrait of London and a visual record of history taking place, charting the ravages of the Second World War and the subsequent rebuilding process, followed by the construction booms of the 1980s and more recent years in Docklands and the City. The amount of scaffolding and the number of cranes we see chart the change in progress; if these same views were photographed in two years' time, London would look different again.

But this book, like London itself, is as much a story as a history. The captions accompanying the photographs do not try to catalogue the buildings that have come and gone but instead tell the stories that surround them. They provide many hard facts about the city but, more important, they are a treasure-trove of anecdotes – quirky, odd, macabre, trivial. And there are answers to questions that you would probably never think of asking, such as, who coined the phrase 'only ten more shopping days to Christmas'? Which novelist invented the pillar box? Where did the brothers Cadbury get the idea for milk chocolate? Which hotel created the peach Melba? Where did Shell Oil get its name?

Over London will introduce you to snooker-playing nuns, Hokey-Pokey Men, and a young lady on horseback who cut people's kite strings with a pair of shears. It will also tell you where some of London's most famous visitors have stayed, including Casanova, Emperor Haile Selassie, Dvořák and Walt Disney. And the book reveals a few secrets, such as the connection between the terrorist Carlos the Jackal and Cherie Blair; why there are only six dials at Seven Dials; why Chelsea Harbour is not in Chelsea, and Kensington Gardens are not in Kensington; and how John Major came to live in Brixton.

This is a book that will delight and amaze, a fascinating snapshot of London at the turn of the millennium, freeze-framed while the city marches on into the future. The sparkling new Millennium Wheel that appears in some of these pictures will one day be as distant a reminder of the millennium celebrations as the Royal Festival Hall is of the 1951 Festival of Britain. New landmarks will age: the Dome may become as familiar an old friend as Tower Bridge, provided it is not torn down; Canada Tower at Canary Wharf will be superseded by taller buildings; scaffolding and cranes will move on. Today, Jason Hawkes' images are a marvel of modernity. In the future, they will be a reminder of the way things were; in another eighty years, they will be as old as the old pictures are now, and it will be time to photograph them all over again.

An early Aerofilms sortie, 1919, below; Jason Hawkes, far right, with pilot Ian Evans, 2000.

The CITY

The City is where London began. Throughout its history it has been growing and changing but never more so than in the eighty years between these sets of photographs. Although it is no longer enclosed by a stone wall, the City is still in many ways separated from the rest of London by its unique customs and traditions. It has a Lord Mayor, Beadles, Sheriffs, Aldermen and its own police force, and some of the ancient traditions are embodied in the buildings shown in the photographs that follow, such as the Guildhall, Mansion House and Livery Company Halls.

The skyline of the City has changed drastically since the early pictures were taken. While the Bank of England and the Royal Exchange survive as historical reminders of the City's financial might, it is modern landmarks, such as Tower 42 (formerly the NatWest Tower) and Richard Rogers' Lloyd's Building, that symbolize the fact that the City is still at the heart of Britain's banking, insurance, investment and mercantile services.

The City stretches from Temple Bar in the west to the Tower of London in the east – an area of 677 acres, which gives rise to the City's other name: the Square Mile. This ancient part of London is steeped in history, myths and legends, the strangest of which concerns Bladud, an ancient king of Britain, who crash-landed a magical flying stone on the site of St Paul's!

Few buildings remain from the City's distant past, as four-fifths of it was burnt to the ground in the Great Fire of 1666, but the twisting convolution of narrow roads and streets, which can be seen from the air, predates the Fire; Christopher Wren's grand plan for a new layout of wide avenues was lost in the rush as people hurriedly rebuilt their property on the old road layout.

St Paul's Cathedral is the City's most famous landmark, and the most prominent of the buildings to rise from the ashes of the Fire. It still dominates even the modern pictures, although the other City churches and the Monument have all but disappeared beneath the tide of office blocks.

Since the Great Fire, the City has been rebuilt several times: a Victorian construction boom and the arrival of the railways resulted in the skyline seen in the photographs of the 1920s, evoking the austere atmosphere of bowler-hatted commuters streaming in and out of the City. The massive changes since then are due to the huge amount of reconstruction required after the Blitz and to a frenzy of office-building in the 1980s; during Mrs Thatcher's era the image of the City was that of young high-fliers spending their days in the money markets and their nights in champagne bars, leaving a legacy of thrusting steel-and-glass monuments to commerce.

CANNON STREET 1921

The population of the City of London fluctuates widely, from the six thousand who live there to a workforce of more than 360,000, many of whom arrive at and depart from Cannon Street Station, seen in the foreground of both pictures. The station appears far more imposing in the older picture, with its spectacular single-span were over forty in one square mile. Like St Paul's, the majority of these churches were rebuilt by Christopher Wren after the Great Fire of London in 1666, and many of them can still be seen in the later picture, peeping out between the office buildings that have grown up around them. The closest church to Cannon Street Station is St Michael Paternoster Royal, which, despite its name, has no royal connection: 'Royal' is a corruption of 'Reole', once a nearby street inhabited by vintners who imported wine from La Reole near Bordeaux.

Both photographs show a new bridge. Southwark Bridge had been rebuilt just before the 1921 picture, and in the modern picture work is in progress on the Millennium Bridge, the first bridge to be built across the Thames in London since Tower Bridge was opened in 1894.

ST PAUL'S CATHEDRAL 1921

The world-famous dome of St Paul's Cathedral caused as much controversy in its day as the Millennium Dome, built three hundred years later. A dome was thought to be unsuitable for an English cathedral, and the church authorities wanted a traditional spire. However, Christopher Wren, the

architect, perservered with his vision and created an icon that still characterizes the City skyline in the twenty-first century.

Dickens described Wren's masterpiece as 'the most conspicuous building in London', and the older photograph shows how St Paul's still totally dominated its surroundings early on in the twentieth century. The modern view reveals the tremendous power of Wren's design. Despite the fact that the encroaching office buildings have diminished the scale of the cathedral, its awesome presence still makes it the centre of attention. On the ground it is easy to forget that there is more to St Paul's than the dome, which noses its way between the surrounding buildings, but seen from the air, the grace and beauty of the cathedral's cruciform shape become apparent.

The most notable ceremonies to have taken place there since the Second World War are Sir Winston Churchill's funeral and the wedding of Prince Charles and Lady Diana Spencer.

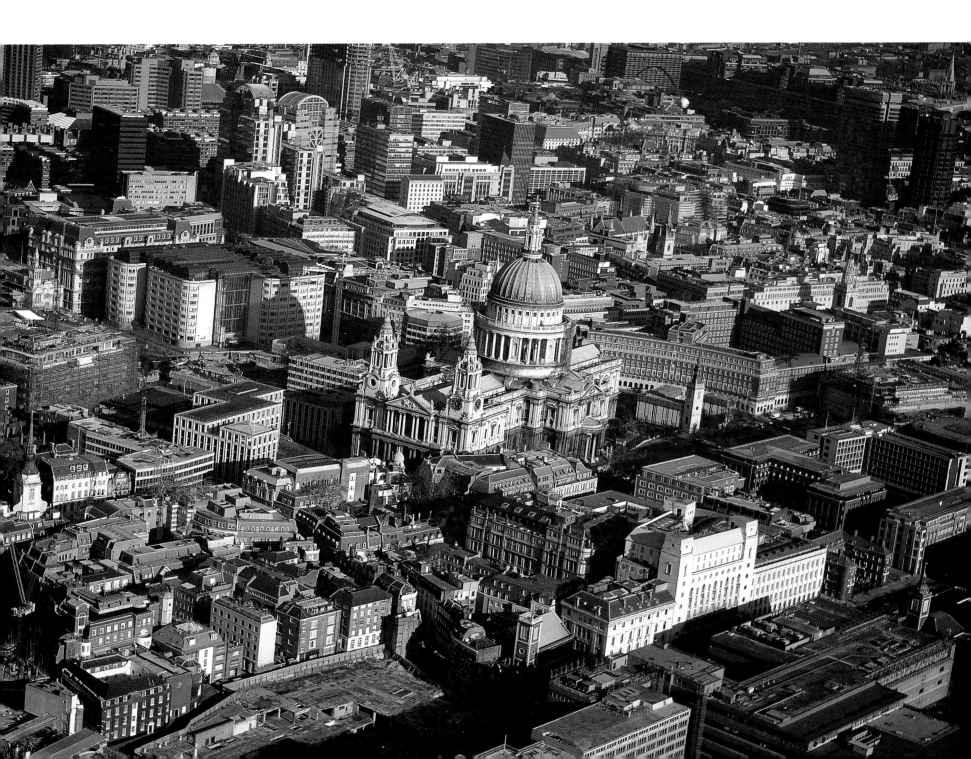

ST PAUL'S CATHEDRAL 1950

St Paul's, which rose from the ashes of the Great Fire of 1666, became a symbol of hope and defiance for Londoners during the Second World War. The older photograph illustrates how miraculous it was that the cathedral remained unscathed amidst the devastation caused by the Blitz ten years earlier: seventy-six consecutive nights of bombing, interrupted only on 2 November 1940 when bad weather grounded the Luftwaffe. The modern picture shows how the City was rebuilt on a grand scale after the destruction of the war, and how many of the buildings that survived the Blitz were later demolished in the name of progress.

To the north of St Paul's is Paternoster Square, which was destroyed in air raids along with around six million books and the bookshops for which the area was renowned. The replacement buildings were ugly and unpopular, and in the later picture the square is, again, being demolished for redevelopment. North of Paternoster Square is Wren's Christ Church, which has remained a hollow shell since the war and is now a rose garden, with only its tower intact. Behind the church is the National Postal Museum, which includes the first pillar box, invented by novelist Anthony Trollope in his day job as Post Office Surveyor.

The smaller dome to the north-west of St Paul's is the Central Criminal Court, better known as the Old Bailey, where many infamous trials have taken place, including those of Oscar Wilde, Dr Crippen and the Yorkshire Ripper. The court was built in 1903–6 on the site of the notorious Newgate Gaol, whose most famous inmate was Casanova.

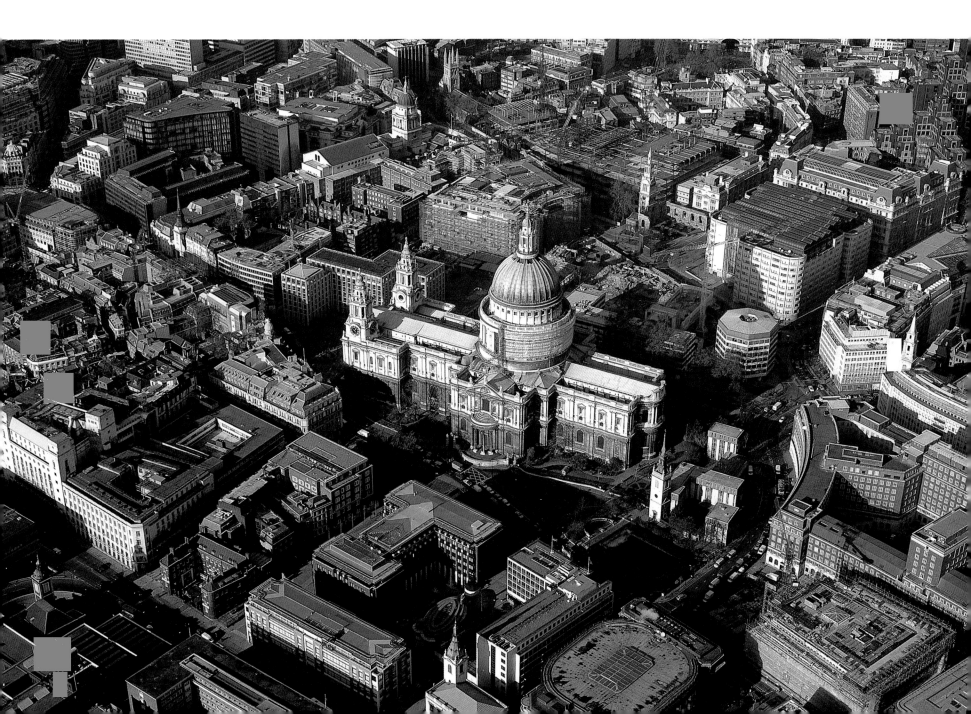

THE BANK 1937

Although physically overshadowed by modern tower blocks, three grand old buildings at the centre of these photographs – the Bank of England, the Royal Exchange and the Mansion House – still encapsulate the City and what it stands for. 'The Old Lady of Threadneedle Street', as the Bank of England is affectionately known, was established during the reign of William III to raise funds for the war against France. The City's roots as a

centre of world commerce are even older: a 'bourse' was opened by Elizabeth I, who disliked the word and decreed that it was 'to be proclaimed the Royal Exchange, and so to be called from henceforth and not otherwise'. Across the road from the Royal Exchange is the palatial Mansion House, the official residence of the Lord Mayor of London during his or (on

only one occasion, so far) her term of office. Immediately south of Mansion House is the church of St Stephen Walbrook, Wren's 'dress rehearsal for St Paul's'. Its central dome can be seen in both photographs.

This part of the City also has a curious association with toilets: Sherborne Lane is said to be a corruption of the medieval word

'shitteborwe', or 'shitborough', meaning public toilet. One of Dick Whittington's innovations as Lord Mayor was to build a unique 128-seat public toilet, which was flushed by the Thames! In 1855, the first cistern-operated public toilets were opened outside the Royal Exchange, but they were for gents only; ladies had to cross their legs until 1911.

FENCHURCH STREET 1934

Fenchurch Street Station has all but disappeared from the later photograph, hidden between and beneath the proliferation of office buildings that sprang up in the second half of the twentieth century. Fenchurch Street was the first station to be built within the City walls, and it was rebuilt in 1935, a year after the earlier photograph; the office development that now surrounds the station appeared in the 1980s. Until 1849, trains were dragged by cable as far as Minories, from where they had to make it to Fenchurch Street under their own momentum; they left helped by the force of gravity, needing 'only a slight push from the platform staff'.

The Tower of London has been a fortress, a palace, a court of justice and a prison. It has also served as an observatory, an armoury, a mint, and, before the word 'zoo' was coined, a menagerie. The only remaining animals are the famous ravens, which have their wings clipped to guard against the prophecy that if the ravens leave the Tower, the monarchy will fall.

Surrounded by trees in the older photograph and marooned on a bleak traffic island in the new stands the Church of All Hallows. A close look shows that the spire has changed in the later picture, because only the red-brick tower survived the Blitz. This is the same tower that Samuel Pepys climbed in 1666 to survey 'the saddest sight of desolation' after the Great Fire.

SMITHFIELD MARKET 1953

Smithfield was once 'a plain grassy space just outside the City Walls'; its name is a corruption of 'smooth field'. This unremarkable patch of open ground has, over nine centuries, been a horse fair, a venue for sporting events and royal tournaments, the site of St Bartholomew's Fair, a jousting arena and a public execution

ground: criminals were hanged here, witches burned, boiled or roasted alive, and hundreds of Protestants burned at the stake during the reign of 'Bloody' Mary.

Smithfield is now London's biggest meat market, covering ten acres. For several hundred years, live cattle were herded into the City and slaughtered here. The livestock often stampeded, sometimes taking refuge in shops; this is thought to be the origin of the phrase 'a bull in a china shop'. Eventually the live cattle market was moved to Islington and new market buildings were erected at Smithfield, which can be seen in both pictures. In 1958, the poultry section burnt to the ground, and the replacement market hall was completed five years later. Smithfield Market employs about 1,500 people, sells 150,000 tonnes of meat a year, and has its own police force and licensing hours: from 6.30 a.m. you can buy breakfast and an early morning pint.

TOWER BRIDGE 1927

A skyline prickly with church spires tells as much of a story as the aeroplane or the steamships on the River Thames. Most of the churches still stand in the later picture, but they are obscured by the buildings that have grown up around them.

The Tower of London marks the eastern edge of the Square Mile, and was actually built outside the City walls by William the Conqueror, to keep an eye on the inhabitants within. Today the roles are reversed, and it is the City that looms over the Tower. Tower Bridge was designed to be in architectural harmony with its ancient partner, and has a stone-clad steel frame, to support the weight of the great lifting arms of the roadway, known as 'bascules' after the French word for see-saw.

In the 1920s picture, monuments to God dominate the skyline; eighty years later they are dwarfed by monuments to commerce. The steel and glass of the modern towers of London speak of the financial might of the City, in particular the sleek black Tower 42 (formerly the NatWest Tower), built on the site of the house of Thomas Gresham, financial adviser to Elizabeth I and founder of the Royal Exchange. The Lloyd's building in front of it was designed by Richard Rogers, architect of the Millennium Dome. The porters at Lloyd's of London still wear waiters' livery, a reminder of the company's origins as a coffee house.

The WEST END

The West End today is synonymous with the theatre, but it is also famous for its museums, galleries, restaurants and shops. Being the nearest thing London has to a centre, 'West End' seems an odd name: west of what, and why 'end' when it lies at the heart of a city defined by north and south circular roads and encircled by a motorway? The answer lies with London's origins; when the Square Mile had no more room for development, the city spread east and west along the Thames. The most fashionable areas were to the west, where the streets, squares and public buildings gave the West End the shape and character we see in these pictures.

These photographs buzz with life: the older ones were taken just before the changes that swept away the last of the music halls, and they reflect the atmosphere that led to the nostalgic celebration of the West End in the First World War song *It's a Long Way to Tipperary*, with the words 'goodbye Piccadilly, farewell Leicester Square'. The modern images resound with the hustle and bustle of Oxford Street and Trafalgar Square, and the roar of traffic on Park Lane and Hyde Park Corner. Heavy traffic is nothing new, though: just seven years after the earlier pictures, Hyde Park Corner was declared the world's busiest junction, and in 1931, traffic rationalization on Oxford Street banned horses and slow-moving vehicles! Traffic has wrought many of the changes seen during these eighty years, with Park Lane, Hyde Park Corner and Piccadilly Circus newly laid out, the Aldwych just being built, and Marble Arch being detached from Hyde Park until, in the modern picture, it is merely the centrepiece of a roundabout.

New landmarks have appeared, such as Centre Point, the BT Tower and the rebuilt Royal Opera House, and old ones have been extended and updated: Broadcasting House is brand new in the older pictures, while Bush House and Selfridges are half built. The Houses of Parliament, Buckingham Palace, Trafalgar Square and Westminster Abbey, meanwhile, remain unaltered, highlighting the vast changes taking place around them. Westminster is a city in its own right and is almost as ancient as the City of London. The first palace at Westminster was built by King Canute, and every monarch since William the Conqueror has been crowned at the Abbey, except for Edward V and Edward VIII, neither of whom was ever crowned.

The cranes and scaffolding in many of the recent photographs show that London is still changing: for example, the dome of the reading room at the British Museum, the country's oldest public museum and host to many great thinkers, is being modernized to inspire the minds of the twenty-first century.

PALACE OF WESTMINSTER 1921

This stretch of river marks the boundary between the Borough of Lambeth and the ancient City of Westminster, which was once a river island. Lambeth, to the right of the picture, has changed almost beyond recognition, while Westminster Abbey and the Palace of Westminster remain unaltered except for being cleaned and repaired after bombing raids by the Luftwaffe during the Second World War.

The first palace at Westminster was built by King Canute, and it was on this reach of the Thames that he famously tried to stop the tide. The current palace, with the familiar sight of Big Ben, is the home of Parliament, where there are an amazing thousand rooms linked by two miles of corridors. Directly across the river from Big Ben is St Thomas's Hospital, which was rebuilt extensively after the war; the later picture shows that Lambeth Palace Road was re-routed to make way for the new buildings.

Changes have also occurred on the river itself, with the arrival of the Millennium Wheel and, less obviously, the rebuilding of Waterloo Bridge. The original bridge, visible in the older picture, was described by Parliament as 'a work of stability and magnificence', but in 1923, two of the piers settled and a temporary bridge had to be built alongside. Both were demolished in 1936 and replaced by the present bridge; the architect was Sir Giles Gilbert Scott, who also designed Battersea Power Station and the traditional red telephone box.

EMBANKMENT 1921

The Victoria Embankment is an often unnoticed but quite amazing feat of engineering: towards the end of the nineteenth century, thirty-seven acres of land were reclaimed from the river by building a wall that extended more than four metres below the low-water mark and six

metres above the high. The buildings stand where the river bank once was, and the water at high tide would have covered the area where the roadway and gardens are now.

The Embankment is home to London's oldest monument, Cleopatra's Needle, and to one of London's most famous hotels, the Savoy (the second building from the right). To the left of the Savoy, the Hotel Cecil has been replaced by Shell Mex House, and next to that the Adam brothers' famous Adelphi terrace was replaced in 1936–8 by the Adelphi Hotel. 'Adelphi' is Greek for brothers, and refers to Robert, James and William Adam, who built the original terrace.

The Savoy Hotel stands on the site of the medieval Savoy Palace, on land still owned by the Duchy of Lancaster. The hotel was built by Richard D'Oyly Carte, alongside his Savoy Theatre, and quickly became known as London's grandest hotel. Cesar Ritz, after whom the Ritz Hotel was named, was its first manager; Guccio Gucci, founder of the famous Italian fashion house, started out as a dishwasher there; and guests included Monet, who painted the Thames from one of the south-facing rooms, Sarah Bernhardt, who nearly died there, and Dame Nellie Melba, for whom the hotel created the peach Melba.

BUCKINGHAM PALACE 1921

Green Park and Buckingham Palace Gardens have emerged relatively unscathed from the traffic management schemes of the 1960s, but Hyde Park Corner, seen in the foreground of the recent photograph, below right, has completely changed since the 1921 picture. The Palace gardens, where the royal garden parties are held each summer,

are separated from Green Park by Constitution Hill, which was named not after a written constitution, which England has never had, but after the constitutional walks that Charles II used to take there.

Buckingham Palace has been the official residence of the British monarch for a surprisingly short time, in fact only since 1837, when Queen Victoria moved in. Known as Buckingham House, it was upgraded to a palace for George IV, although he did not survive long enough to live in it. The palace was designed as a three-sided open court, with Marble Arch providing a grand entrance. However, the courtyard was later enclosed by the famous east façade, which now faces The Mall, and Marble Arch was removed to its present position at Cumberland Gate.

George V was on the throne at the time of these early photographs. He was succeeded by Edward VIII, who was once seen jumping out of a palace window and running away across the garden, to avoid a confrontation with his private secretary!

The Palace was hit nine times by German bombs during the Second World War, prompting Queen Elizabeth, now HM The Queen Mother, to remark: 'I'm glad we have been bombed; I feel I can look the East End in the face.' It was while he was inspecting air-raid damage across the country that her husband, George VI, conceived the idea of the George Cross and the George Medal, to be awarded for civilian heroism.

HYDE PARK CORNER 1921

At first glance the devastation caused by the traffic schemes of the 1960s does not seem too great, but look again at Constitution Arch, once connected to Green Park and now isolated on a traffic island, with six lanes of tarmac cutting across Buckingham Palace Gardens. Hyde Park

has fared even worse, and the damage is more obvious in the picture on page 33 than in this foreshortened view. In 1921, Park Lane followed the line of the buildings and was narrower than the tree-lined curve of the park ring road, but in 1960–3 that curve became one carriageway of Park Lane, and the corner of the park was turned into a huge roundabout.

Of all the buildings that stood close to Cumberland Gate only Apsley House survives, with its famous address: No. 1 London. It was the home of the Duke of Wellington and is now the Wellington Museum, run by the Victoria & Albert Museum. The house was handed to the nation on the proviso that the family could remain in residence; the current Duke still has

a flat on the ground floor. Constitution Arch, originally known as the Wellington Arch, was erected as a memorial to the Iron Duke; the sculptor of the equestrian statue that now graces the top of the arch but is hidden by scaffolding in the recent picture, held a dinner for eight of his friends inside one of the horses shortly before completing the work!

PICCADILLY CIRCUS 1921

Piccadilly takes its name from the ruffs, or 'pickadills', worn by the dandies who used to promenade here in the seventeenth century; the circus did not appear until two hundred years later, when it was built to form the intersection of Piccadilly with the newly built Regent Street.

It was effectively a crossroads but, as the 1921 picture clearly shows, the buildings on the corners had concave curved frontages that formed a circular place, or circus. The symmetry of this arrangement was, however, destroyed in the 1880s to make way for Shaftesbury Avenue.

The famous illuminated signs first appeared at the turn of the century; the buildings facing directly on to Piccadilly Circus were presented with lucrative advertising opportunities and exploited the new technology of flashing, electrically lit signs, which have been a feature of Piccadilly Circus ever since.

Eros is probably the world's most frequently misnamed statue; it is, in fact, the Angel of Christian Charity. Designed as a memorial to the philanthropist Lord Shaftesbury, the statue is thought to be a visual pun because there is no arrow, or shaft, in the angel's bow, which is pointing at the ground; and is the shaft buried?

TRAFALGAR SQUARE
1921 & 1927

'Sir, we have gained a great victory but we have lost Lord Nelson' was how the news of Britain's greatest naval triumph was delivered to the First Secretary of the Admiralty in 1805. Improvements to the Charing Cross area took place in 1830, and

the resulting public square was named to commemorate the Battle of Trafalgar. Soon after, the forty-four-metre-high column was erected and a statue of Nelson placed on top. The First Secretary would not have been amused by rumours nearly two hundred years later that the European Union had decreed that Trafalgar Square and Waterloo Station be renamed to appease the French.

Trafalgar Square has changed little since the 1920s, except that the fountains are now much paler; they were remodelled in 1939 and lined with blue tiles to give light and colour to the water. Embankment Place, incorporating Charing Cross Station, was designed by Terry Farrell. It was completed in the 1990s and looks like an enormous juke box standing on the north side of Waterloo Bridge.

ALDWYCH 1921

The distinctive crescent of Aldwych was created in 1905, but the
construction of buildings to line the new road was quite slow to follow:
the early photograph shows large gaps to the north, with Bush House

still under construction. Bush House was completed in three stages – in 1923, 1930 and 1935 – and it has been the home of the BBC World Service since 1940. For this reason it is thought of as thoroughly British but it was in fact built by an American, Irving T. Bush. The inscription 'To the Eternal Friendship of English-Speaking Nations' refers not to the BBC's lofty ideals but to a businessman's wish for accord between Britain and the US.

The church stranded in the middle of the road to the south of Aldwych is St Mary le Strand. It is crumbling due to the combined effects of age, weather, a wartime bomb and heavy traffic, but in happier days Charles Dickens' parents were married there. Further south still, part of Somerset House can be seen; in the modern picture the courtyard is undergoing renovation, having once again become a public space since the departure of

the Inland Revenue. At the top of the picture is the London School of Economics, whose famous alumni include Mick Jagger, Cherie Blair and the terrorist Carlos the Jackal.

LEICESTER SQUARE 1921

Cinema moved into Leicester Square in the 1930s, but by the time of the 1921 photograph it was already a popular place for entertainment, boasting theatres such as the Alhambra, Empire, Hippodrome and Daly's. Most of the buildings surrounding the famous square have

COVENT GARDEN 1938

Covent Garden was once a garden belonging to a convent, hence the name. The land was mainly pasture, but after the Dissolution of the Monasteries in the sixteenth century it was built on and became a

luxury neighbourhood 'fitt for the habitacions of Gentlemen'. The piazza was laid out in the seventeenth century by Inigo Jones, who was inspired by the Piazza d'Arme in Livorno, Italy.

Although the familiar twin roofs of the market hall were not built until the nineteenth century, Covent Garden fruit and vegetable market started in 1656 and continued until 1974, when it relocated to Nine Elms in Battersea. The north-eastern corner of the piazza is dominated by the Royal Opera House, eighty years old in the older picture and just rebuilt in the new.

Opposite the Royal Opera House is Bow Street Magistrate's Court, famous for the magistracy of novelist Henry Fielding, author of *Tom Jones*, who set up the city's first police force: the Bow Street Runners. What Henry Fielding would have made of the treatment of future authors here is not known: in 1895, Oscar Wilde was incarcerated here after his arrest for 'committing indecent acts', and in 1928, Bow Street magistrates banned Radclyffe Hall's lesbian novel *The Well of Loneliness*.

HOLBORN 1937

Holborn is named after High Holborn, the road that runs across the top of both pictures and which, in turn, takes its name from the Holebourne, a tributary of the River Fleet, which is now covered over. The tree-filled square of Lincoln's Inn Fields is part of Holborn: Lincoln's Inn is one of the legal Inns of Court, whose alumni include Sir Thomas More, Oliver Cromwell and Margaret Thatcher.

Long Acre was once a narrow strip of market gardens cultivated on a long acre of land. It was Covent Garden's main street years before the market hall was built; and perhaps its greatest claim to fame is that John Logie Baird created the world's first television studio at No. 133 during the 1920s. Long Acre runs through the middle of both pictures, towards the temple-like edifice of the Freemasons' Hall, which was just four years old in the early photograph.

This is the headquarters of the United Grand Lodge of England, and was built as a memorial to masons who died in the First World War.

To the left of both pictures is Seven Dials, the meeting point of seven streets, marked by a column topped with six tiny sundials; the seventh dial is said to be formed by the column itself surrounded by the circular roadway. The column does not appear in the 1937 picture because the original had been torn down in

1773 after a false rumour that there was money buried at its base. A replica was unveiled in 1989, and there is a plaque nearby explaining how to convert sundial time to Greenwich Mean Time or to British Summer Time. The plaque was sponsored by one of Covent Garden's more famous residents: Dave Stewart of the Eurythmics.

BRITISH MUSEUM 1921

Montagu House in Bloomsbury was bought as a home for the British Museum after Buckingham House, now Palace, proved too expensive. The museum's origins lie with Sir Hans Sloane, the wealthy Chelsea doctor after whom Sloane Square is named, who had amassed a collection of over eighty thousand curios, which he

bequeathed to the king for £20,000. The king declined the offer, so Parliament bought the collection and set up a foundation to house it, resulting in the world's first public museum.

To house the expanding collection, the museum was rebuilt as a large quadrangle with an open courtyard in 1823–47. Only five years later, in 1852, this was converted into the Reading Room, beneath whose dome have sat the likes of Thomas Carlyle, George Bernard Shaw, Lenin, who worked at desk L13 under the pseudonym of Jacob Richter, and Karl Marx, who wrote *Das Kapital* at desk O7. At the time of the later picture, the museum was undergoing a £100 million redevelopment, following the departure of the British Library to St Pancras.

As well as effectively founding the British Museum, Hans Sloane invented milk chocolate; while physician to the Governor of Jamaica, he became the first person to mix milk with cocoa, and he sold his recipe to the Cadbury brothers.

TOTTENHAM COURT ROAD
1921 & 1946

Tottenham Court Road was originally a market road leading to Tottenham Court, a popular place of entertainment, situated to the north of what is now Euston Road. When the furniture store Heal's was first

biggest bookshop, at the top of the picture. William and Gilbert Foyle opened their original shop in 1904. After failing their Civil Service examinations and advertising their textbooks for sale, they realized what a market there was for such books. The existing Foyle's building was inaugurated by the Lord Mayor of London in 1929. Regular customers included George Bernard Shaw, Sir Arthur Conan Doyle, Noël Coward and Walt Disney, who was often seen browsing among the art books.

established at No. 196 in 1840, the land was still so rural that the lease provided for 'the proper accommodation of forty cows at least'; the cowsheds burned down in 1877.

Directly opposite Heal's is Whitefield's Memorial Chapel, which, in its day, was the largest Nonconformist church in the world, seating over seven thousand people; it was nicknamed 'Whitefield's soul trap'. Further north, across the massively redeveloped junction with Euston Road, is the National Temperance Hospital, founded as an experiment to determine whether alcohol, prescribed as a matter of course in hospitals, really did have therapeutic powers. The routine prescription of alcohol did not end until 1939!

St Giles Circus, at the southern end of Tottenham Court Road, became known as such in 1921, and is now marked by the 1960s skyscraper Centre Point. The aerial perspective is deceptive because St Giles-in-the-Fields, visible only in the modern picture, has stood unaltered since it was founded in 1733.

South of St Giles Circus is Charing Cross Road, with Foyle's, until recently London's

LANGHAM PLACE 1931

Although the gleaming white Portland stone of Broadcasting House was painted battleship grey during the
Second World War, a German bomber still managed to find its target. But when the bomb was dropped on
the evening of 15 October 1940, Bruce Belfrage, with stiff upper lip, continued to read the *Nine O'Clock News*
through the blast. The building was restored to pristine whiteness after the war, and still dominates Langham

Place today, taking up the entire block, with its 1960s extension to the north.

Queen's Hall is visible in the older picture, next to the distinctive circular portico of the Church of All Souls, but it was destroyed in 1941; St George's Hotel now stands on the site. In 1895, Henry Wood formed the Queen's Hall Orchestra, and Queen's soon became London's premier concert hall. After it was bombed, Sir Henry's promenade concerts moved to the Albert Hall, where 'the proms' are still held.

Facing Broadcasting House is the Langham Hotel, which appears in several Sherlock Holmes stories. Guests of the original Langham Hotel included Toscanini, Dvořák, Mark Twain, Arnold Bennett, and the exiled emperors Napoleon III and Haile Selassie. It was bombed during the war (one blast shattered the 38,000-gallon water tank, causing enormous damage) and re-opened in 1991 as the Langham Hilton, after repairs costing £80 million.

OXFORD STREET
1925 & 1939

Oxford Street is probably the most famous shopping street in the world, but things might have been different if any of its previous names – The Waye from Uxbridge, Acton Road or Tyburn Way – had stuck. The road does lead to Oxford, but the name was only consolidated in

the eighteenth century when the second Earl of Oxford acquired land to the north of the street.

Oxford Street cuts a two-mile swathe through the West End, following the route of the Roman road from Hampshire to Suffolk. Closed-circuit television protects today's shops and shoppers, but one eighteenth-century traveller described the street as 'a deep hollow road and full of sloughs; with here and there a ragged house, the lurking-place of cut-throats'.

Shops along Oxford Street today include Marks & Spencer, which started life as Marks's Penny Bazaar in 1884. Michael Marks was a Polish immigrant, who came up with the slogan 'Don't Ask the Price – It's a Penny' to get around the fact that he did not speak English. In 1894, he went into partnership with Thomas Spencer, establishing market stalls all over England; in 1926, M&S became a public company, and in 1938, it opened its first Oxford Street store.

SELFRIDGES 1921

Harry Gordon Selfridge came to London from Chicago, to make his fortune. His dream was to create a department store that stretched from Oxford Street to Wigmore Street, with a dome as big as St Paul's; he almost achieved the dream, save for the dome. Selfridges was the largest building ever designed as a single shop, although, as the early photograph shows, construction did not take place all at once. The store

opened for business on 15 March 1909 in what was just one corner of the building that would eventually become an Oxford Street landmark. The first item sold was a handkerchief for 1s. 4d, to a Madam Barry of Bond Street.

By 1921, demolition had begun at the western end of the block, and on 31 August 1927, The Chief, as Selfridge was known, laid the coping stone, sealing the gap between the original building and the western extension. Further expansion wiped a road off the map: the name Somerset Street can still be seen carved into the building where the street now forms the entrance to the loading bay. The famous Ionic columns appear much whiter in the older picture, although they were cleaned in 1980.

Between 1921 and 1980, Selfridge pioneered many retailing 'firsts'; these included the bargain basement, in-store credit and the first sale of a television set. But there is one thing that will outlive all his other achievements, including the building itself: Harry Gordon Selfridge coined the familiar phrase 'only ten more shopping days to Christmas'.

MARBLE ARCH
1922 & 1956

Marble Arch once formed the triumphal entrance to Buckingham Palace, but it was moved to Cumberland Gate when the east façade was added to the palace. At first, the Arch was within the boundary of Hyde Park, but successive traffic schemes have left it isolated in what is, effectively, a giant roundabout. In 1922, Marble Arch appears very grand, as part of a processional route; by 1956, it was becoming overshadowed by new buildings, and in the modern

pictures it looks quite forlorn. In the earliest picture, the Church of the Annunciation, seen top right, was only eight years old; in the later pictures, just the spire peeps out from behind the massive bulk of the Cumberland Hotel.

The Odeon appears as a façade in 1956, its pairs of Corinthian pillars matching those of the hotel next door; the present uninspiring building went up in 1967. Further left on Hyde Park Place is the Tyburn Convent, home of a Benedictine order, which recently hosted the first Nuns' World Snooker Championships.

Three rooms at the top of Marble Arch were used as a police observation post until 1950. During a riot in 1855, a detachment of police emerged from the arch, as from the Trojan Horse, much to the surprise of demonstrators; Karl Marx was among the crowd and thought it was the start of the English Revolution.

changed since 1921, and even the layout of the distinctive gardens at its heart, still rather grandly known as Leicester Fields, has been altered. The square was originally residential, but this changed when hotels, shops and museums moved in. By Victorian times, the area was celebrated for its Turkish baths, oyster houses, theatres and music halls.

The square was almost entirely rebuilt between the wars; the AA headquarters took over the west side, work beginning just two years after the earlier photograph, while, to the north, the Empire Music Hall was demolished in 1927 and replaced a year later by the Empire Cinema. The Warner Cinema now stands on the site of Daly's. On the east side of the square the

minarets of the Alhambra, originally the Royal Panopticon of Science and Art, were replaced in 1936 by the sleek black lines of the Odeon.

Ten years after the Alhambra music hall opened in 1860, it had problems renewing its licence after Wiry Sal raised her foot 'higher than her head several times towards the audience and had been much applauded'.

EAST LONDON and DOCKLANDS

The East End is the stuff of legend: Jack the Ripper and the Whitechapel murders; the Kray Twins; the Elephant Man; the Battle of Cable Street. To the south and flanking the river is Docklands, once the gritty heart of London as a busy and thriving port.

The physical changes in these two areas – massive slum clearance and the redevelopment of redundant docks – are some of the most far-reaching in the book, reflecting the enormous social shifts that have taken place: successive waves of immigrants have added their character to the East End, and an entire way of life on the docks has ended.

The photographs of Shoreditch and Whitechapel show the effects of the arrival and disappearance of the railways, the damage done during the Blitz, which left gaps like missing teeth, and the appearance of exotic buildings, such as the East London Mosque, while those of Bethnal Green illustrate how the clearance of overcrowded Victorian slums has created more open space and green areas.

In Docklands, the changes have been even greater: the 1905 *Baedeker Guide* described the busy life of the docks: 'Nothing will convey to the stranger better the vast activity and stupendous wealth of London than a visit to these warehouses, filled to overflowing with interminable stores of every kind of foreign and colonial products.' In the 1920s pictures, the Thames is seen packed with barges and the quaysides are teeming with steamers and freighters, but by 1980, it had all been shut down: in the modern photographs the vast empty expanse of the docks looks like a watersports centre waiting to be opened.

The London Docklands Development Corporation was set up in 1981, since when most of the changes have taken place. One hundred per cent tax relief on capital expenditure, no business rates for ten years and no planning controls attracted huge investment. This led to the establishment of the Docklands Enterprise Zone and to the development of Canary Wharf, where tomatoes and bananas were once landed from the Canary Islands, hence the name. Olympia and York, a Canadian company, financed the construction of the skyscraper Canada Tower, forever destined to be misnamed Canary Wharf. It is Britain's tallest building and perhaps London's most famous modern landmark after the Dome.

SHOREDITCH 1938

Shoreditch is scarred with a twisting pattern of roads and railway tracks, but it has the ancient roads to thank for its existence: the village grew up at the junction of the Roman roads of Old Street and Kingsland Road, close to where the tall white spire of St Leonard's stands out at the centre of both pictures. St Leonard's dates from the twelfth century, and the village stocks and whipping post still stand in the churchyard.

The railways arrived in Shoreditch, left their mark and disappeared again; the tracks that cut right through the 1938 picture have now gone, leaving a strange flat-topped embankment. The route once served Broad Street Station, which in its day was London's third busiest terminus, but it was finally closed in 1984 to make way for the Broadgate office development. A passenger train from Liverpool Street Station can be seen in the modern picture, winding its way through a cutting south of the warehouses on the bottom right, which are built on the site of another defunct station, Bishopsgate.

Hoxton Square, to the left of both pictures, was built in 1683 and was the first urban development in Shoreditch. Now it is at the centre of the area's regeneration as a trendy, arty enclave. Arty associations are nothing new, though: Richard Burbage opened the country's first theatre here in 1576, imaginatively called The Theatre. It was later dismantled and rebuilt in Southwark as The Globe.

WHITECHAPEL 1921

Whitechapel lies at the heart of London's old East End. Steeped in history, myth and legend, it is probably most famous for Jack the Ripper's Whitechapel murders and the shooting for which Ronnie Kray was sent to prison. Whitechapel's rich cultural heritage is derived from the various ethnic groups that have settled here over the years.

The French Huguenots, among them the Courtauld family, were the first immigrants in the seventeenth century, and their arrival introduced the word 'refugee' to the English language. Famous for their textiles, they established Petticoat Lane market; in 1830, the authorities renamed it Middlesex Street, but the original name has stuck.

Next came the Irish, who, paradoxically, built many of the area's Protestant churches, to be followed by the Jews, whose most famous moment was the Battle of Cable Street, when Mosley's Blackshirts were prevented from marching through the area. The Jewish legacy includes schools, synagogues, Harold Pinter and Vidal Sassoon. Most recently, Whitechapel has become home to a large Bengali community, whose influence can be seen in the appearance of the copper dome of the East London Mosque at the top of the modern photograph.

Whitechapel Road is also home to the Whitechapel Bell Foundry where the world's most famous bells have been cast, including the Bow Bells, America's Liberty Bell, Big Ben, and the 'oranges and lemons' bells of St Clement's, as described in the nursery rhyme. Close by is the Royal London Hospital, where Joseph Merrick ended his days after Dr Treves discovered him being exhibited as the 'Elephant Man' in a freak show.

BETHNAL GREEN 1936

At one time, Cambridge Heath Road actually led to a heath, but the village of Bethnal Green became overcrowded as early as the seventeenth century, with the expansion of the silk-weaving industry from Spitalfields. Throughout the centuries, social observers have found overcrowding and poverty here: 'three or four families in a house', 'poverty as few can conceive without seeing it,' and, a hundred years later, in 1889,

'forty-five per cent of the population living below subsistence level'. The Victorians attempted to improve the situation, but the 1936 photograph shows that the area remained hopelessly overcrowded. By the time of the later picture, the clearing of slums and the building of council estates has resulted in a little more breathing space for the inhabitants.

One improvement effected by the Victorians was the establishment of Victoria Park, shown top right. Dickens described it as being 'very prettily laid out… with various appliances for amusement… Victoria-pk is one of the things which no student of London life should miss seeing'. The modern commentator Iain Sinclair is more acerbic: 'St Agnes' Gate and the "green lung", the idealized version, the salvation of dust-choked, slum-dwelling proles, is pictured on a board… a homage to the dominant ethic, the great green god. I like the park, visit it most days, circle it like a prison yard, but I'm increasingly uneasy about the way it presents itself. The park has begun to feel it is better than we are. Regimented flower beds are back.'

ST KATHARINE'S DOCK 1946

The story of St Katharine's goes back almost as far as that of its neighbour, the Tower of London. In 1148, the Royal Foundation of St Katharine was established here, dedicated to the saint who was tortured on a spiked wheel, and after whom the Catherine wheel is named. The Foundation's church survived the Reformation, the Great Fire of London and the Gordon riots, only to be demolished in 1825, to make way for the docks designed by Thomas Telford. His revolutionary design of linked east and west basins provided an exceptional length of quayside for a relatively small enclosure of water. The docks flourished but suffered appalling damage during a daylight bombing raid by the Luftwaffe on 7 September 1940; the older photograph shows the extent of the damage, with all the warehouses around the East Dock completely razed. After the war, the docks fell into decline, and they were closed in 1968; a year later work began on developing the luxury marina that has replaced the industrial quays and warehouses. The centrepiece of the new St Katharine's Dock is Ivory House, which is the only surviving warehouse from Telford's docks and which, in its heyday, handled not only ivory but perfume, wine and shells. Legend has it that the founder of a certain multinational used to collect discarded scallop shells here, which provided the name and logo for his organization: Shell Oil.

WAPPING 1922

There are one or two clues that reveal these pictures are of the same place: the shape of Wapping Sports Centre matches the curved quays of the old Wapping Basin, and the Pier Head still exists, although the lock is now just a slipway. A close look shows that the grand Regency houses on East Pier and West Pier are the same in both photographs: they were

built as homes for officials of the London Dock Company. Further east, many of the warehouses have survived, now converted into apartments. One of them incorporates the original overhead gangways that still cross Wapping High Street.

St John's Church seems to be a survivor from the old picture, but it is, in fact, a new building. Only the tower survived the Blitz, after which the church was rebuilt; it has since been converted into apartments.

WAPPING 1949

When London Docks opened in 1805, with the destruction of many of Wapping's houses,

they were the nearest docks to the City, originally handling tobacco, rice, wine and brandy,

and later, sheepskin, cork and molasses. The twenty-acre Western Dock was the largest of the group, with Wapping Basin providing a river entrance to the south. Western Dock was linked to the smaller, seven-acre East Dock by the narrow spit of Tobacco Dock, and then to the Thames via Shadwell Basin. All of these docks can be seen in the old photograph but only Shadwell Basin survives today; it can be seen to the right of the modern picture. The London Docks were eventually closed in 1969 and filled in for redevelopment.

The magnificent four-storey warehouses that lined the docks stood above a labyrinth of brick-vaulted wine cellars, which now form part of the headquarters of Rupert Murdoch's News International. Often referred to as Fortress Wapping, it can be seen at the centre of the later picture. Alongside, the Tobacco Dock warehouses have been converted into a self-styled 'Covent Garden of Docklands', but they remain eerily quiet because the enterprise went

bust before it got off the ground. Just across the road, to the north, are the white walls of Nicholas Hawksmoor's church of St George in the East, a burnt-out shell in the post-war photograph but a unique conversion in the modern one: part of the building has been made into apartments, while a tiny church has been built in the space of the original nave.

MILLWALL 1934

Millwall is named after the mills that used to stand on the marsh wall and help drain the low-lying Isle of Dogs, of which it is part. The mills were demolished in the nineteenth century to make way for the industry, docks and shipyards that became the lifeblood of the area; Brunel's *Great Eastern* was built in a Millwall shipyard. Millwall Dock opened in 1868 and handled mainly bulk grain arriving from the Baltic; some of the grain silos can be seen in the 1934 photo. The dock had its own railway system and was later linked with West

India Dock to the north, but all the docks were closed in 1980, and eight thousand jobs dwindled to just six hundred. Since then, new life has been breathed into the area by the Docklands Development Corporation and the establishment of the Enterprise Business Park, which is visible in the modern photograph on the north side of the dock.

The large grassy area to the left of the picture is Mudchute, formed by silt dumped after the dredging of Millwall Dock; the railway cuts across the corner of Mudchute to Island Gardens, where Christopher Wren used to sit and contemplate his masterpieces – the Royal Naval College and the Old Royal Observatory – which are still visible across the river.

The name Millwall is perhaps best known as a football club. Although its home has been south of the river since 1910, the club is thought to have its origins in the factory team from Morton's canned food, based at Millwall.

RIVER LEA 1924

The Lea snakes its way towards the Thames, past industrial units and gasometers, on the final leg of its journey from Bedfordshire; it is hard to imagine that over a thousand years ago King Alfred's ships pursued the Danes up this same river. Once the boundary between Middlesex

and Essex, the Lea has recently been cleaned and now supplies one-sixth of London's water.

The lowest reach of the Lea flows past Canning Town, where it is known as Bow Creek; the town is thought to be named after Lord Canning, a Governor-General of India, and was developed to house workers on Victoria Dock, which is just visible in the modern photograph. The Thames Ironworks & Shipbuilding Company was established on Bow Creek in 1846, where it produced about nine hundred warships for the British and foreign navies. It closed in 1912.

In the foreground of the modern photograph, the terraced houses and industry of Bromley-by-Bow have been cleared to make way for the northern approach to the Blackwall Tunnel. The tunnel's capacity was increased with the opening of the southbound tunnel in 1967; the southbound carriageway now passes beneath the Millennium Dome, which can be seen at the top of the picture.

EAST HAM

1933

The first person to be buried in the East Ham Jewish Cemetery was a young able-bodied seaman who died on 6 January 1919 while on active service, and was buried here six days later, close to the trees on the northern boundary; his grave is marked by a box privet that is as old as the cemetery itself.

By the time the earlier photograph was taken in 1933, the cemetery had started to fill up with closely packed graves; at the end of the millennium, it looks full to capacity. At its centre, the synagogue keeps a watchful eye over this peaceful graveyard, which from the air is a moving reminder of the passage of time. The factory has been replaced by tower blocks, but the Norman church, just visible at the bottom of both photographs, remains the same, as it has done for more than eight hundred years.

SILVERTOWN 1921

With the exception of the broad sweep of the Thames and the two huge drums at the point where the river bends, everything about Silvertown has changed since 1921, yet it still looks the same;

with its heavy industry and the curve of North Woolwich Road matching that of the river.

Silvertown seems an overly romantic name for such an industrial part of the riverside, but it is not as fanciful as it sounds: the area was first developed in the 1850s around the rubber and telegraph works of S.W. Silver and Co. By the time of the earlier picture, industry here included chemical, gas, varnish and petrol works – a volatile combination that four years

earlier had resulted in the 'Silvertown Explosion', when fifty tons of TNT exploded at Brunner Mond's chemical works.

Henry Tate & Sons built a sugar refinery here in the late nineteenth century, and Abram Lyle opened the Plaistow Wharf Refinery less than a mile away in 1882. The two companies were competitors until they amalgamated in 1921; their main refinery is still at Silvertown. Sir Henry Tate is also famous as the benefactor

of the Tate Gallery. The modern-day commentator Iain Sinclair draws a parallel: 'I always think of the gallery on Millbank as twinned with the belching treacle factory at Silvertown, a long haul downriver... no one should be allowed to gawp at the Stanley Spencers, or lift the felt from the cases of Blakes, until they have completed a tour of inspection at Silvertown, licked sugar crystals from the web of their fingers.'

ROYAL DOCKS 1924

These photographs document a startling change, from crowded quaysides to still waters, from docks and cranes to the empty runway of London City Airport. Until the eighteenth century, ships in the port of London were unloaded midstream by flat-bottomed barges known as

lighters; they were so called because they literally made the ships lighter. Enclosed docks, such as the Victoria, Royal Albert and King George V, which make up the Royal Docks, became necessary because so much was stolen from ships in port: thieves would strip them right down to their anchors, 'scuffle-hunters' would filch unguarded wares from the quayside, and 'mudlarks' would collect goods that had been thrown overboard by accomplices from the water's edge. Huge losses led to the formation of the Marine Police Force – now the Thames Division of the Metropolitan Police – and to the establishment of docks, such as the Royal Albert, seen to the left of these pictures, and the King George V to the right.

Sadly, the Royal Docks closed in 1981, and the airport was opened in 1987. To limit the level of aircraft noise, planning permission stipulated that only Dash 7 planes could use the airport, with a maximum of 30,160 flights per year.

ROYAL DOCKS 1952

The world has moved on since the photograph above was taken almost fifty years ago. In 1952, ships packed the quaysides of the largest dock system in the world, but by the turn of the century, the docks have been closed, the quays replaced with the runway of London City Airport, and the Thames Barrier and the Millennium Dome have appeared in the background. Together, the Royal

Docks make up the largest area of impounded dock water in the world: they cover 245 acres, and there are nearly nine miles of quay, which once handled bulk grain and, later, frozen meat, fruit and vegetables. During the General Strike of 1926, there was a near crisis when strikers threatened to cut off power to the docks, which would have destroyed three-quarters of a million refrigerated carcasses. Eventually, the navy came to the rescue, coupling together the generators of two submarines, to provide the necessary power for the refrigeration.

ROYAL DOCKS 1968

A view of the Royal Docks from the west, with Victoria Dock in the foreground; this was the first of the three Royal Docks to be built, and was opened by Prince Albert in 1855. Soil from the excavation of Victoria Dock

was used to consolidate the marshes of Battersea Fields, in order to create Battersea Park, which opened four years later.

Victoria Dock was such a success that it was extended to the east, to form the Royal Albert Dock, which is the largest of the three, although the aerial perspective makes it look smaller than the Victoria in both pictures. King George V Dock was begun in 1912, but the First World War delayed work and it was not opened until 1921, as the Royal South Albert Dock. Although the smallest of the three, it was still able to accommodate the cruise liner *Mauretania*, which docked there in 1939. Only sixty years after the last of the Royal Docks opened, all three were closed: the London Docklands Development Corporation bought them from the Port of London Authority, and subsequently supported a proposal for the building of London City Airport, which was opened in 1987.

NORTH, WEST and SOUTH

London initially developed in what is now the City. The name comes from the Celtic 'Llyn-dun', often translated as 'the hill by the pool', and the Tower of London is a lasting reminder of the strategic importance of Tower Hill, by the Pool of London. It was the Pool that led to London's development as a port, and as the city expanded it spread east and west along the Thames. As we have seen, this led to the development of the West End and the East End. Since then, development and urban spread has been along more predictable lines: outwards from the centre, giving Greater London the circular shape it has today.

The previous chapter looked at the eastern sector of this circle; this chapter will examine the remaining quadrants in turn, working anti-clockwise around the city, and ending with London's most famous millennial landmark, the Dome at Greenwich.

Seen from the air, the suburbs to the north, west and south have their own individual characters. Some areas look the same today as they did eighty years ago, for example, Putney, Hampstead, Blackheath and Notting Hill, while others, such as Hammersmith, Crystal Palace and White City, are barely recognizable.

Again we see the genesis of some of London's most familiar landmarks: Battersea Power Station being built and then dismantled; the growth of London Zoo and Harrods; the appearance of the Thames Barrier and Chelsea Harbour; and the disappearance of the Crystal Palace. Many of London's sports grounds and exhibition halls lie slightly out from the centre, and this chapter charts the demise of White City as well as the expansion of Lord's, Wimbledon, Olympia and Earl's Court.

Traffic plays its part in the changing cityscape: away from the centre, buildings tend to be lower, and white lines, zebra crossings and traffic lights are more obvious; in some cases these are almost the only changes that have taken place. But elsewhere, there are dramatic changes: in Hammersmith an entire road has been built since the older picture, with the Hammersmith flyover visible as an ugly scar right through the middle of the modern view.

And this chapter ends where the first one began; with a dome. While the domes of St Paul's and the Tower of London tell the story of old London, the Millennium Dome and Canada Tower usher in the new.

KING'S CROSS 1921

The name King's Cross commemorates a monument to George IV, which once stood at the crossroads close to the site of the station. It was the biggest station in England when it opened in 1852, and was said to 'wear a magnificent appearance', so much so that the chairman of the Great Northern Railway was accused by his shareholders of extravagance. He replied that it was 'the cheapest building for what it contains and will

contain, that can be pointed out in London'. Dickens described it as 'externally hideous but inwardly commodious'.

The Grand Union Canal cuts across the tracks to the north of the station and then disappears into the 305-metre Islington Tunnel; at one time the boatmen had to lie on their backs with their feet on the roof of the tunnel and 'walk' their barges through.

The Battlebridge Basin, filled with colourful narrow boats in the later picture, is lined with warehouses, one of which was built by the Italian entrepreneur Carlo Gatti as an ice house. In the nineteenth century, ice had to be collected from rivers and lakes, then stored underground in specially constructed ice wells. Eventually, due to pollution and demand, London's ice had to be imported, but the first

consignment melted while Customs Officers tried to decide what duty to charge on it!

Gatti was also responsible for introducing ice cream to London; he supplied most of the city's ice-cream sellers, who were known as 'Hokey-Pokey Men' after their street cry 'Ecco un poco', meaning 'Just try a little'.

EUSTON STATION 1936

These photographs show the oldest and the newest of London's main line stations. The 1936 picture is of the original Euston Station, built in 1837 for the London and Birmingham Railway; the journey to

Birmingham took five hours, and trains had to be pulled up the hill from Camden Town by winding cable as the steam engines did not have enough power. The station had a grand portico and booking office, with hotels to each side; the expense was justified by the company's claim that the entrance to the station would 'necessarily become the Grand Avenue for those travelling between the Midland and Northern parts of the kingdom'. Ten years later the Great Hall was opened and became known as 'the second splendour of Old Euston'. But in 1963, it was all demolished, to make way for the spectacularly ugly modern terminus, which was opened by Elizabeth II in 1968. Times had changed, and British Rail announced that 'simplicity is the keynote in the design of the new Euston'.

When Euston Road, which runs in front of the station, was first planned as the New Road in 1756, the Capper family, who lived on the south side of the proposed route, petitioned against it to Parliament. They complained that the clouds of dust raised by driven cattle would spoil their hay. The eccentric Capper sisters were described thus: 'They wore riding habits and men's hats. One used to ride after boys flying kites with a pair of shears to cut the strings. The other seized the clothes of those who trespassed to bathe.'

LONDON ZOO 1946

London Zoo opened to the public in 1828 and was immediately inundated with visitors: thirty thousand in the first seven months. The rules of the 'zoological gardens' stipulated that whips were to be left at the gate but ladies were permitted to carry their parasols, although they had to be restrained from poking the animals with them through the bars. In more enlightened times, the zoo is a major centre for research, presenting itself as a saviour of species under threat of extinction.

The zoo initiated several world firsts, including the world's first aquarium, insect houses and reptile house; in an attempt to charm a cobra, one reptile keeper was bitten between the eyes and died hours later. The zoo also made its mark on popular culture: the abbreviation 'zoo' was coined by a music hall singer; the original logo for Penguin Books was sketched at the penguin pool; and when a giant panda arrived in 1938 it prompted an immediate craze for cuddly panda toys.

Across the road from the zoo is Primrose Hill, still divided into allotments in the older photograph; these were created as part of the war effort, to reduce the need for imported food. At one time, Primrose Hill was known as Greenberry Hill. It is said that the magistrate hearing evidence relating to the Popish Plot was found dead in a ditch here, and that servants by the names of Green, Berry and Hill were convicted and hanged for his murder.

HAMPSTEAD 1938

Hampstead has been an exclusive and sought-after area since 1698, when springs with supposedly medicinal properties were discovered; and has more blue plaques celebrating famous residents than any other London borough. The village's attraction as a spa is commemorated in street names such as Well Walk and Flask Walk, although the Vale of

Health was actually a malarial swamp until the late eighteenth century.

Part of Hampstead's continuing attraction is its proximity to the heath, which is fortunate to have survived the nineteenth century: the Lord of the Manor, Sir Thomas Maryon Wilson, introduced fifteen parliamentary bills in an attempt to win permission to build on it.

Dickens found the heath far too busy for his tastes, and complained 'nor do the donkeys so plentifully provided for the delectation of 'Arry and his young lady add much to the aesthetics of the scene'.

Hampstead has been home to poets, playwrights and novelists, but the resident with perhaps the most famous literary connections

lies in the cemetery: the Hungarian Laszlo Bíró, who invented the ballpoint pen in the year the earlier photograph was taken. Bíró's invention had far-reaching consequences for the twentieth century: a product designer for Mum used the principle to create a giant ballpoint for the application of deodorant, and thus the roll-on was born.

LORD'S 1921

Lord's is the world's most famous cricket ground, home of the MCC, the Ashes, and a stuffed sparrow that was 'bowled out' by Jehangir Khan in 1936. In the early days, the grass was kept short by sheep, which were penned in on match days; later, a visiting tribe of Native Americans set up camp on the turf, and during the Second

stations to be built, and certainly the most
modest, in part because the Great Central
Railway was short of money after legal battles
with the MCC and local residents over building
the last few miles of track into London.

The Great Central Hotel, built at the same
time as the station, has been redeveloped so
that its open courtyard is now enclosed under a
glass roof. Meanwhile, the white Town Hall and
St Mary's Church, with its semi-circular portico
and cylindrical tower, remain unchanged.

The copper dome and minaret of the London
Central Mosque stand out to the right of the
later photograph. First mooted in the 1920s, the
mosque was not completed until 1978. Its
oriental architecture is a suitable addition to a
park that was laid out for the Prince Regent
(later George IV), whose most celebrated artistic
project was the Brighton Pavilion.

KNIGHTSBRIDGE 1949

Legend has it that two knights fought to the death here on a bridge across the Westbourne River, since dammed to form the Serpentine, visible at the top of the picture; a less romantic theory about the origin of the name is that it is a corruption of Neyt, an adjoining manor.

Taking up an entire block at the centre of both pictures is Harrods; the most noticeable change to the store is the appearance of a helicopter landing pad in the later photograph.

Charles Henry Harrod was a wholesale tea merchant who took over a small Knightsbridge grocer's shop in 1849. His son, Charles Digby Harrod, bought the shop from his father and built up the business: among the early account customers were Oscar Wilde, Lillie Langtry and Ellen Terry. The store was bought by House of Fraser in 1959, but it became a family firm once more in 1985 when the Fayed brothers purchased it for £615 million.

In 1898, Harrods installed the first-ever escalator in London, and stationed attendants at the top of it, to hand out smelling salts and brandy to nervous customers! Three years later, work began on the famous terracotta façade, which, a century later, is lit every night by 11,500 lightbulbs.

TATE GALLERY 1949

The most notable change on Millbank in the fifty years that have passed since the earlier picture is the appearance of Millbank Tower. Built in the 1960s, it is now the headquarters of the Labour Party. Next door is the Tate Britain, which opened in 1897 as the National Gallery of British Art, using money donated by the sugar magnate Sir Henry Tate,

who also gave his collection of sixty-five paintings and two sculptures.

The gallery has been extended several times since its opening, the most recent addition being the Clore Gallery, which was built in 1987 to house the Turner Bequest. Turner is widely regarded as Britain's greatest artist, and he bequeathed over one hundred paintings to the nation. He exhibited his first watercolours in the window of his father's barbershop in Covent Garden while still a boy, and at the Royal Academy when he was fifteen. His relatives added to the bequest, so that the Turner collection at the Tate is the largest in the world, with over three hundred paintings and an amazing nineteen thousand drawings and watercolours. The gallery also sponsors the annual, and usually controversial, Turner Prize.

Now that the Tate's modern art collection has been moved to Tate Modern on Bankside, the Millbank site has officially re-opened as Tate Britain.

Sir Henry would no doubt be delighted that the name Tate is associated with art galleries and that of his partner Lyle with golden syrup, but both of them will go down in history as inventors of the sugar cube.

SLOANE SQUARE 1928

Sloane Square is named after Sir Hans Sloane, the wealthy doctor whose curios formed the basis of the British Museum. In the 1980s, the square gave its name to the 'Sloane Rangers', the most famous of whom was Lady Diana Spencer.

One of London's 'lost' rivers, the Westbourne, flows under the east side of Sloane Square and is carried over the tracks of the tube station in a large iron pipe. The station was bombed in November 1940, and restoration took eleven years to complete. Bombing also destroyed the Royal Court Theatre, which was rebuilt in 1952; prior to that, many of George Bernard Shaw's plays had opened there under his own direction. In 1956, the Royal Court became the home of the English Stage Company. After closing for three years for refurbishment, which cost £25 million, the theatre re-opened in February 2000.

On the other side of Sloane Square is Peter Jones; the shopfront awnings of the 1920s photograph have been replaced in the later one by Britain's first glass curtain wall, the façade of a new building that was built from 1932–6. The son of a Welsh hat manufacturer, Peter Rees Jones set up a successful draper's business that sadly fell on hard times after his death in 1905. Early the following year, John Lewis walked to Sloane Square from his shop in Oxford Street with twenty £1,000 bank notes in his pocket. He bought the business outright and it has been part of the John Lewis Partnership ever since.

KING'S ROAD, CHELSEA
1934

In *Nicholas Nickleby*, Dickens describes Cadogan Place – the leafy rectangle in the top left of the photographs – as the connecting link between 'the aristocratic pavements of Belgrave Square and the barbarism of Chelsea'. On the Chelsea side of this divide are Sloane

Square and King's Road, which was originally built as a private road, so that Charles II could avoid the traffic on his way to Hampton Court Palace. George III later used the road to travel to Kew. The road was eventually made public in 1830; until then, ordinary people could use it only on production of a copper pass stamped 'The King's Private Roads'.

The green area to the south is the Duke of York's HQ, originally a school for soldiers' orphans and now the home of the Territorial Army and the regimental HQ of the Royal Corps of Signals. Militarism is slightly at odds with the area's fashionable image, for which it was famous in the Swinging Sixties, when the likes of David Bailey, Mick Jagger, George Best and the 'Chelsea Set' would hang out in the various boutiques and coffee bars. In the 1970s, King's Road became the birthplace of punk when designer Vivienne Westwood and her boyfriend of the time, Malcolm McLaren, joined forces with Sid Vicious and Johnny Rotten. In the twenty-first century, the road is still famous for its cafés, boutiques and antique shops.

The Laura Ashley shop was once the premises of Thomas Crapper, renowned for his water closets. His name has also made a fundamental contribution to the English language.

CHELSEA HARBOUR 1932

Lots Road power station dominates the foreground of the older picture, belching smoke from all four chimneys

as it generates power for London Underground. This huge power station originally provided electricity for the

District Line, and was built in the face of vociferous opposition, the irony being that Chelsea is almost devoid

of tube stations. Since then, the power station's capacity has been increased, with the removal of two chimneys in 1963, when it was converted from coal-burning to oil-burning. Between them, Lots Road and Greenwich power stations now supply two-thirds of the electricity required for the entire underground network. At one time, there were plans to re-equip both stations, so that they could provide more power than London Transport would need, which would allow them to sell the surplus to the National Grid.

In the modern picture Belvedere Tower stands at the river entrance to the Chelsea Harbour complex, with a ball attached to the needle on its gold-coloured roof, showing the height of the tide. In the 1980s, P&O and Globe bought twenty acres of industrial wasteland in front of the power station and built Chelsea Harbour, which they describe as a 'unique world of houses, flats, offices, restaurants and

shops and a luxury hotel around a working yacht harbour'. Chelsea Harbour is actually a misnomer, though, because the boundary of Chelsea is formed by Chelsea Creek, which runs just to the south of the power station. This means that the entire Chelsea Harbour complex lies not in Chelsea but in Fulham.

KENSINGTON GARDENS 1929

The area on the left of the modern picture became known as Albertropolis in recognition of Prince Albert's role in establishing the museums there. Today, his name is usually associated with the Albert Memorial and the Royal Albert Hall, at the centre of both photographs. A 999-year leasehold of seats, set up to finance the

construction of the hall, is still in place, and entitles the owners to free attendance at every performance; Queen Victoria bought twenty seats, which make up the present Royal Box.

The Albert Memorial was designed by George Gilbert Scott, the architect of St Pancras Station. Throughout its history, the Memorial has been loved and hated with equal passion. Although Queen Victoria never expressed her opinion, Scott did receive a knighthood.

Kensington Gardens, to the right of the photograph, were once the gardens of Kensington Palace, although, confusingly, the gardens are not actually in Kensington: the border with Westminster runs across the top of the picture, separating the Palace from the Round Pond. The Palace itself is divided into a number of apartments, which are allocated to various members of the royal family. This led the Duke of Windsor, formerly Edward VIII, to refer to it as 'the aunt heap'.

KENSINGTON 1922

St Mary Abbots is London's tallest parish church, and dominates even the two huge 1930s Art Deco department stores that have appeared across the road in the later photograph. The store closest to Kensington

Gardens is Barker's Arcade; the company took over Derry & Toms next door in 1920, and then embarked on an enormous rebuilding programme that resulted in these two colossal stores. On the roof of the Derry & Toms building, now subdivided into a number of different organizations, are the famous Kensington Roof Gardens, which, at one-and-a-half acres, are the largest roof gardens in Europe. There are three themed areas: an English woodland garden with mature trees and a stream, a Tudor garden with walled courtyards, and a Spanish garden with a mock-convent, complete with bell tower and well. The Sun Pavilion is now used as a night club and is run by Richard Branson's Virgin Group.

Just behind these two monolithic buildings is Kensington Square, which became an extremely fashionable address after royalty moved into Kensington Palace in 1689: William Thackeray wrote *Vanity Fair* at No. 16, Edward Burne-Jones lived at No. 41, and Hubert Parry, who wrote the music to William Blake's *Jerusalem*, gave music lessons to Ralph Vaughan Williams at No. 17. John Stuart Mill lived next door in the house where the first volume of Thomas Carlyle's manuscript for *The French Revolution* was accidentally used by the maid to light the fire.

EARL'S COURT 1936

The village of Earl's Court expanded and became built up after the arrival of the railway, which cuts across both of these photographs. The graceful semi-circle of Philbeach Gardens and the crescents opposite survive, although many of Earl's Court's grand houses were subdivided into bedsits or used as hotels after the First

World War. The recent transient population of antipodean backpackers has earned Earl's Court the nickname Kangaroo Valley.

The first exhibition space in the area was the Empress Hall, seen west of the railway in the older photograph; its curved roof is echoed in the architecture of Earl's Court 2, which was opened by Princess Diana in 1991 and which extends out over the tracks in the modern picture. The main building is under construction in the earlier picture and opened in 1937 with an exhibition of chocolate and confectionery. At the time it was the largest reinforced concrete building in Europe, covering an area of twelve acres.

Another new arrival since the 1930s is the grandly named Empress State Building, at the centre of the picture. Recently abandoned by the Ministry of Defence, it is due to re-open as a hotel in 2002. To the left, the Brompton Cemetery remains undisturbed. Those laid to rest here include the suffragette Emmeline Pankhurst, Keats' lover Fanny Brawne, and Samuel Sotheby, who founded the famous auction house. Just off the bottom right corner of the picture is the former home of Earl's Court's most famous resident: Freddie Mercury.

NOTTING HILL 1921

With the exception of a couple of buildings, such as the block opposite the church, very little has altered here since 1921; the most significant changes seem to be the road markings and the amount of traffic.

When these Victorian crescents were first laid out, the area was still known as the Potteries (after the Kensington Gravel Pits and the potteries, which were situated just to the west of the picture), or as the Piggeries, alluding to the three-to-one ratio of pigs to people in Notting Hill. By the 1950s, the area was described as 'a massive slum, full of multi-occupied houses, crawling with rats and rubbish', a contributing factor to the country's first race riots in 1958. The Notting Hill Carnival began unofficially the following year in response to the riots, and it is now the biggest street festival in the world outside of Rio.

St John's Church, built on what was once part of the Hippodrome racecourse, marks the crest of Notting Hill. Spectators watched from where the church is today, while horses raced around a course that circled the base of the hill.

WHITE CITY 1933

There seems to be something missing from the modern photograph…
White City's vanishing stadium was built for the 1908 Olympics, the
memorable year that Pietri did not win the Marathon, although he was
the first runner to enter the stadium. He was so exhausted that once

inside the stadium he started running in the wrong direction, stumbled and fell. He then received medical attention and a helping hand from the stewards before crossing the line still well ahead of the other runners, but he was disqualified. However, his courage won the hearts of the nation, and he was awarded a special gold cup by Queen Alexandra.

Earlier in 1908, the strange collection of buildings seen in front of the stadium were laid out for the Franco-British Exhibition. There were forty acres of white-stuccoed buildings (from which White City takes its name), half a mile of waterways and a Court of Honour with a lake and illuminated fountains, surrounded by Indian-style pavilions. The grounds were

taken over by the London County Council in 1936, to build the council housing seen in the modern picture. Meanwhile, the stadium continued to be used for sporting events. Greyhound racing was introduced in 1927, and from 1931–3, White City became the home ground of Queen's Park Rangers. Sadly, the demolishers moved in towards the end of 1984.

WOOD LANE
1937

Two bridges – one carrying the Hammersmith & City Line over Wood Lane, the other carrying an access road over the tracks of the Central Line to the goods depot – are the only indication

that these pictures are of the same place. In the older picture, Wood Lane is busy with trams, cars and pedestrians on their way to the White City stadium. Many of the pedestrians would have been walking from the now-disused Wood Lane tube station, which opened on the Metropolitan Line to serve the Franco-British Exhibition. Two platforms were added in 1920 when the Central Line was extended northwards, but the station proved unsuitable for Central Line trains, so, in 1947, a second station was opened on Wood Lane: the present White City station, seen in the modern picture.

Wood Lane station then reverted to being a Metropolitan Line station only. It closed in 1959.

After the Second World War, the BBC acquired thirteen-and-a-half acres of the site used for the Franco-British Exhibition and built their new home there: Television Centre. These new studios were first used in 1960, twenty-four years after the BBC's first regular broadcasts began from studios at Alexandra Palace. The new, seven-storey, circular main building on Wood Lane has several blocks radiating outwards from it, and it was massively extended to the north in the 1990s.

OLYMPIA 1921

Olympia has expanded dramatically since 1921, but the original hall at its heart is still recognizable. It opened in 1884 as the National Agricultural Hall, and changed its name to Olympia two years later. The buildings were

taken over by the War Office during the First World War. Additions since the 1921 picture include the National Hall, built two years later, and the Empire Hall, built in 1929.

Shortly after its opening, Charles Dickens commented on the building's 30-metre-high glass roof, which he said 'presents a marvellously light and airy appearance… so graceful are the lines that it is difficult to realize that the iron is sufficiently strong to ensure safety from the heaviest winds'.

Dickens went on to say that Olympia was 'available for cattle, horse, poultry, dairy, dog, and implement shows… there are to be national and international exhibitions, military tournaments, hippodrome performances, horse-racing, trotting matches, foot-races, assaults-at-arms, and athletics generally; theatrical performances, concerts, bazaars, balls, picture galleries, and so on'.

The first Motor Show was held here in 1905, and the first International Horse Show in 1907. It also hosted Cruft's Dog Show from the 1930s, until it moved to the Birmingham NEC in 1991.

HAMMERSMITH 1931

Since Anglo-Saxon times, Hammersmith has been dominated by the roads along which it

developed, a fact that is truer today than ever: the Hammersmith flyover was built in 1961, to

relieve congestion on the Broadway, one of the busiest traffic intersections in London. Together with the shopping mall and the Novotel next door, it has changed the face of Hammersmith.

Hammersmith Broadway evolved as the meeting point of major north–south and east–west routes, and became the focal point of the town with a number of coaching inns, until trains replaced horse-drawn coaches.

Squeezed between the flyover and the railway tracks in the modern picture is the distinctive London Ark, hailed as London's first ecologically-sound building. Designed by Ralph Erskine and built from 1990–1, the interior is flooded with natural light, and triple glazing keeps energy in and traffic noise out. The effect is less successful outside as the noise of the trains reverberates off its exterior curved walls.

KEW BRIDGE 1921

Kew Bridge links Chiswick, in the foreground, with Kew, at the top of both pictures. The first bridge was built in 1749, to replace the Brentford ferry, and had seven wooden arches; the granite bridge in these pictures was completed in 1903. Kew grew up because it was easy to cross the river at Brentford (the island to the right of the pictures is Brentford Ait), and from the sixteenth century, courtiers lived here because it was close to Richmond Palace. Today, Kew is most famous for the Royal Botanical Gardens. Some of its earliest specimens were brought back from the voyages of Captain Cook.

On the other side of the river, Chiswick has something of an identity crisis: it is not known whether the name means 'Cheese Farm' or 'the village by the Stony Beach'.

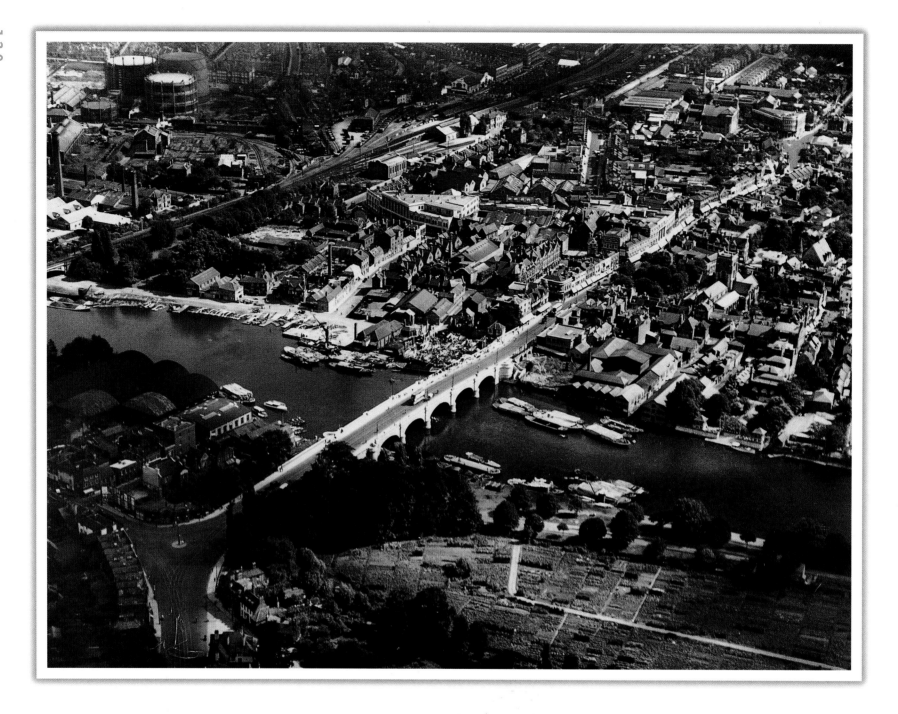

KINGSTON 1928

The huge concrete edifice of the John Lewis store, which straddles the road on the east side of the river, embodies Kingston ancient and modern. The 1980s department store, together with Bentalls and the domed glass roof of the precinct beyond, are part of Kingston's image as a modern shopping centre, while incorporated into the store are the foundations of the twelfth-century bridge that established Kingston's historical importance.

The bridge made Kingston strategically important, but was both a blessing and a curse to the locals: it was a great boon to trade but repairs were a financial burden after frequent damage from floods and civil wars. Tolls were eventually introduced to pay for its upkeep and, until 1750, it was the first bridge across the Thames upstream of London Bridge. The bridge in these pictures was completed in 1828.

Kingston is a Royal Borough whose earliest surviving charter was granted by King John in 1200 in recognition of Kingston's royal history: seven out of the eight Saxon kings were crowned here between 900 and 979. The Coronation Stone stands near Kingston's Guildhall, and marks the place where the kings were crowned. The stone is thought to be part of the ancient throne, and a silver coin from the reign of each king is set into the plinth.

WIMBLEDON 1929

'Wimbledon is a dreary, high, bleak, windy suburb, on the edge of a threadbare heath' –
Virginia Woolf was obviously not as impressed by Wimbledon as the 375,000 tennis fans
who flock here each year to watch the Wimbledon Championships. The tennis
championships have always been played on the courts of the All England Club, which was

originally founded in 1868 as the All England Croquet Club; tennis was not introduced until seven years later. In 1877, the title of the club was changed to the All England Croquet and Lawn Tennis Club, and the first Lawn Tennis Championship was staged. Tennis had been administered by the MCC from Lord's, but new rules were introduced for this competition, and the All England Club has administered the game ever since. Although croquet is no longer played here, the club is still known as the All England Lawn Tennis and Croquet Club.

At the Club's Worple Road ground, the main court was in the centre. When the current Church Road ground was opened by George V in 1922, the name Centre Court was kept, even though it was not a true description. But now that so many new courts have been built, it does once again live up to its name.

Fortunately, the name chosen for the game of tennis by its inventor, Major Walter Clopton Wingfield, did not stick, otherwise all the excitement would revolve around the Wimbledon Sphairistike Championships.

PUTNEY 1938

Putney Bridge is the starting point for what is still rather pompously known as the University Boat Race, despite the fact that only two universities – Oxford and Cambridge – compete. The four-and-a-half-mile course was first used in 1845, long before the present bridge was built, and in Victorian times it was said that

'every tint and shade and film of shade of Gainsborough's *Blue Boy* was patched upon the myriads who covered the Thames Valley from Putney to Mortlake'.

Putney has been described as 'a Victorian–Edwardian suburb': there has been very little development or clearance of housing here since the commuter boom, which started with the arrival of the railway and continued until the First World War. As a result, the 1938 picture looks very similar to the modern one.

Across the river in Bishop's Park is Fulham Palace, which was the home of the Bishops of London from 704 to 1973, since when it has been leased to the Borough Council. The present palace, dating from the sixteenth century, was the largest moated site in England until 1921, when the moat was filled in. Putney Railway Bridge was designed by shipbuilder William Jacomb, Brunel's assistant on the *Great Eastern*, which was built at Millwall.

FULHAM 1935

Before it became built up, Fulham Town was known as 'the great fruit and kitchen garden north of the Thames', with a high street that led to a ferry across the river. By then, Fulham was already famous as the home of the Bishops of London, eight of whom are buried in the churchyard of All Saints Church, seen to the right of Putney Bridge

Approach. Fulham's Grand Theatre, which originally seated an audience of one thousand, used to stand opposite All Saints Church, but it closed in 1934 with the advent of cinema. Bridge House, owned by International Computers Ltd, now stands on the site. On the front of the building is a sculpture called Swan Uppers, which depicts the ancient practice of taking up swans from the river and scoring marks of ownership on their beaks: royal swans were distinguished by five nicks on the bill, two lengthways and three across.

Part of the grounds of the Hurlingham Club, originally established as a pigeon-shooting club, can be seen in the foreground. Pigeon-shooting was abandoned in 1905, and polo became the club's main sport. The rules of the game were formalized in 1875 by the Hurlingham Club Committee, the precursor of the Hurlingham Polo Association, which still retains the name, although the polo grounds (just out of the picture) were compulsorily purchased by the London County Council in 1946 for housing; Sulivan Court now stands on the site.

BATTERSEA PARK 1928

In 1928, Battersea Park would have resounded to the noise of construction work taking place on the enormous Battersea Power Station, which opened just five years later. The park looks unfamiliar without the four great chimneys that now dominate the eastern side. Changes have also taken place within the park; the Festival of Britain Gardens were laid out in 1951, the same year that the Children's Zoo was established, and playing fields, a running track and tennis courts have also appeared since 1928. The Peace Pagoda, which is situated on the riverfront, was built in 1985, a gift from a group of Japanese Buddhists. It is one of seventy such pagodas to be built around the world in the name of peace.

Julius Caesar is reputed to have crossed the river here in the seventh century, but without the benefit of the bridges that now link Chelsea with Battersea; all three bridges in the picture have been replaced since 1928, although it looks as if there are only two. The twin railway bridges were known as Victoria Bridge in the 1920s, and were built for two separate railway companies serving Victoria Station. Now known

as Grosvenor Bridge, they were rebuilt in 1963–7, with the original wrought-iron piers encased in concrete. Chelsea Bridge was seventy years old in the early picture and was replaced with a new suspension bridge in 1934, making it nearly as old in the modern picture as the old bridge was in the early one.

BATTERSEA POWER STATION 1950

The Royal Mail depot at Nine Elms adds a splash of colour to the modern view of Battersea Power Station, which has been described as looking from a distance like an upturned snooker table. This enormous cathedral of power was designed by Sir Giles Gilbert Scott, whose grandfather designed St Pancras Station, and whose own work includes

Liverpool Cathedral and the rather smaller K6 – better known as the red telephone box.

Station A opened in 1933, with a chimney at each end, and was later doubled in size. Station B began operations in 1948 but it was not completed until 1953, three years after the earlier photograph. The vapour belching from the ninety-metre chimneys is a pristine white, having been cleaned of sulphur and other impurities by smoke-washing equipment. Closed in 1983, the empty shell of the power station stands next to the curved scars left behind by the railway tracks of the South Lambeth Goods Depot, now punctuated by a lonely helipad.

Pink Floyd's 1977 album *Animals* featured Battersea Power Station on the front, photographed with a huge inflatable pig attached to one of its chimneys. Legend has it that Hipgnosis, the designers of the cover, did not ask for permission to stage the stunt: the first the authorities knew of it was when a jumbo jet pilot reported it to air traffic control. The story goes that the pig then broke free and was eventually recovered from a Kent garden.

BRIXTON 1949

Brixton followed the pattern of most Victorian suburbs, built up from
open fields within twenty years of the arrival of the railways; the
viaducts can be seen snaking their way across the top of these
photographs. Brixton soon became an important shopping centre, and

Electric Avenue was opened in 1888 as one of the first arcades to be lit by electricity.

After the Second World War, cheap lodging houses attracted a large number of West Indian immigrants, who now define the character of Brixton, with its lively Afro-Caribbean consciousness, trendy bars and thriving market. Brixton is a place of contradictory images.

Often thought of as a black ghetto, the population is, in fact, seventy per cent white, and although the area is seen as cool by 'youthful media types who like a bit of grit in their lives', it does have a bad reputation after the riots there in 1981 and 1985.

Inexpensive accommodation is nothing new to Brixton; that, and easy access to the West

End, meant that from Victorian times this part of south London was a favourite with theatre people. Music hall stars Dan Leno and Fred Karno lived in Brixton at the end of the nineteenth century, and, more recently, former Prime Minister John Major lived here; his father, a music hall and circus performer, had lodgings in Coldharbour Lane.

CRYSTAL PALACE 1928

For those who ever wondered why Crystal Palace is so named, this 1928 photograph gives the answer; incredibly, the whole edifice burned to the ground on the night of 30 November 1936. The blaze was so intense that firefighters were hindered by molten iron and glass, and the combined efforts of ninety fire appliances failed to save the building; the modern picture shows that only the landscaped terraces survived.

The Crystal Palace was modelled on the conservatory at Chatsworth House, and was designed to house the Great Exhibition of 1851. It was originally erected in Hyde Park amidst loud protests from local residents, who thought that the area would become 'a bivouac of all vagabonds' and make Kensington uninhabitable. The park's trees were incorporated into the structure, but so were the sparrows that lived in them; their droppings spattered the exhibits until the Duke of Wellington suggested introducing sparrowhawks.

After the Exhibition, the Crystal Palace was moved to Sydenham where, for eighty years, it formed the centrepiece of a pleasure garden and was used as concert hall, theatre, menagerie and exhibition rooms. Fountains in the gardens were fed by the two ninety-metre water towers seen on either side of the 1928 photograph, and there were also lakes, a cricket ground and a sports arena; several FA Cup finals were played at Crystal Palace between 1894 and the opening of Wembley Stadium in 1923. Two rival plans to resurrect the Crystal Palace are said to be under way: one is a full-scale replica at Sydenham, the other a one-third-size model in Hyde Park.

SOUTHWARK 1921

The London Bridge closest to the camera in the older photograph now spans a lake in Arizona; legend has it that the owners of a theme park in Lake Havasu City thought they were buying Tower Bridge.

The bridge in the modern picture was built from 1967–72. London Bridge Station, at the bottom left of both pictures, was badly damaged during the Second World War, rebuilt in the late 1970s and again refurbished in the 1990s. The tracks from the east are carried over an amazing 878 brick arches, stretching for four miles through Bermondsey, after which they snake off towards Waterloo or curve round on to the Cannon Street Bridge.

The next bridge upstream is Southwark Bridge, completed in 1921 and, therefore, brand new in the earlier photograph. Beyond Southwark Bridge in the modern picture are the beginnings of Norman Foster's Millennium Bridge that now links the City with Bankside. In Elizabethan times, this colourful part of Southwark was known as 'Stew's Bank' for its many 'stewhouses' or brothels; it was also famous for its theatres, including Shakespeare's

Globe, which has been faithfully re-created by American film director Sam Wannamaker. At the top of the modern picture is the former Bankside Power Station, which is now home to London's newest art gallery: Tate Modern.

BERMONDSEY 1946

Bermondsey has a colourful and, by all accounts, smelly past. The name is thought to derive from 'Beormund's eye', meaning island, and the area became famous first for its Cluniac abbey, then for its pleasure gardens, and later as a spa, founded in what is now Spa Road. But the arrival of the railway changed all that and, by

Victorian times, the busy wharves and tenements brought with them some of the worst social conditions in London. Charles Kingsley was horrified: 'Oh God! What I saw! People having no water to drink but the water of the common sewer which stagnates full of… dead fish, cats and dogs', and Dickens commented on 'the unpleasantness of the compound of horrible smells which pervade the whole neighbourhood'.

Since the early picture, when the wharves were still busy with cranes, the docks have been closed down and parts of Bermondsey redeveloped under the Docklands regeneration scheme. West of Tower Bridge demolition has been the order of the day, while to the east many of the warehouses have been restored: Butler's Wharf warehouse, which gives the area its name, has been converted into accommodation, shops and restaurants. Next

door, the old Anchor Brewhouse produced Courage Ales from 1789 until 1982, and was converted into apartments in 1989, retaining the boiler-house chimney at one end and the tower and cupola of the malt mill at the other. Shad Thames (its name is a corruption of St John at Thames), which runs along the back of Butler's Wharf, has also kept its Victorian atmosphere; it was used by David Lynch as a location for his film *The Elephant Man*.

BLACKHEATH 1948

The heath takes its name not from victims of the black death buried here in plague pits, as local folklore would have us believe, but from the black peat that lies beneath the surface. The layout of Blackheath has remained much the same since 1948, although the wartime prefabs and Nissen huts, named after their designer, Colonel P. N. Nissen, have gone.

There is a distinct difference between the bare, windswept heath and the plentiful trees of Greenwich Park, seen to the right of the photographs, while the cityscape beyond the park shows that things have changed elsewhere, even if Blackheath and Greenwich Park have stayed the same.

Legend has it that a Society of Blackheath Golfers was formed here by the Scottish courtiers of James I. This became the Royal Blackheath, the first golf club in England, which amalgamated with Eltham Golf Club in 1923. Blackheath also boasts the oldest open rugby union club in the world: Blackheath FC was formed in 1858, before either the Football Association or the Rugby Football Union, and was one of the founder members of the RFU in 1871. Nowadays kites have replaced golf balls and rugby boots, and Blackheath is renowned as London's premier kite-flying spot.

Blackheath also has its literary associations: John Rokesmith settles here in Dickens' *Our Mutual Friend*, after celebrating his wedding at the nearby Trafalgar Tavern in Greenwich, and in *A Tale of Two Cities*, Jerry Cruncher terrifies the passengers of the Dover coach, who think that he is one of the highwaymen for which the heath was notorious.

GREENWICH 1937

Christopher Wren's Royal Naval College in the foreground of the 1937 photograph is the area's most striking feature. But although it remains unchanged in the modern picture, the eye is immediately drawn to Richard Rogers' Millennium Dome. The twin domes of the Royal Naval College, now part of Greenwich University, are precursors in miniature of the dome of St Paul's; they are also echoed by the domed glass roofs at the entrances to the Greenwich foot tunnel, visible at Island Gardens and Greenwich Pier. The tunnel was completed in 1902 as the replacement for the ferry that had been in existence since the seventeenth century.

An invisible but significant change has taken place close to the Millennium Dome: the southbound carriageway of the Blackwall Tunnel was built from 1960–7 and runs beneath the near side of where the Dome now stands.

Slightly further west, the northbound tunnel is present below the river in both pictures, having been completed in 1897.

It is surprising to see that the *Cutty Sark* is not in the older picture, but the world's last surviving tea clipper only arrived in Greenwich in 1954. Close by is *Gypsy Moth IV*, preserved in dry dock after Francis Chichester's solo round-the-world voyage from 1965–6. Chichester was knighted at the Royal Naval College for his

achievement. Elizabeth II used the same sword that Elizabeth I had used in Greenwich, nearly four hundred years earlier, to knight Francis Drake after his round-the-world voyage.

GREENWICH PENINSULA 1965

The South Metropolitan Gasworks was one of Europe's largest, and in the 1965 photograph, it takes up most of what was once Bugsby Marshes. By the time the Millennium Dome was proposed, a century of industrial use had poisoned the ground, which had to be decontaminated before work could begin.

The second, southbound bore of the Blackwall Tunnel was already under construction at the time of the older photograph. Since then, the heavy industry and the gasholders have been replaced by the spectacular Dome and Norman Foster's impressive transport interchange.

North Greenwich, on the Jubilee Line, is the largest underground station in Europe, capable of handling 22,000 passengers an hour.

The Millennium Dome was designed by Richard Rogers, who was in partnership with Norman Foster until 1967. He is also famous for

the Pompidou Centre in Paris and the Lloyd's building in the City. The Dome at Greenwich is by far the world's biggest, at fifty metres high and over half a mile in circumference.

CHARLTON
1962

Three of London's great modern landmarks are lined up in the picture on the right: the Thames Barrier, the Millennium Dome

and Canada Tower at Canary Wharf. The tower blocks in the distance and the proliferation of industry along the riverside show an enormous amount of development in the forty-odd years that have passed between the two photographs.

The Thames Barrier is a remarkable feat of engineering, with ten movable steel gates; each of the four main gates is as high as a five-storey building, as wide as the opening of Tower Bridge, and weighs over three thousand tonnes. The steel machine housings are the tip of the

iceberg: the actual gates lie in concrete sills on the riverbed and take thirty minutes to raise.

The oasis of green at the centre of the modern picture was excavated in 1915, revealing a hill fort dating from Roman times; the monument was destroyed shortly afterwards by quarrying and now forms Maryon Park. To the left of the park, Charlton Athletic's ground has been modernized since 1962; the area's other football team took its name from the Royal Arsenal at Woolwich but moved to Highbury in 1913.

INDEX

acknowledgements

Ian Harrison:
Raymond Bateman, Harbour Master, St Katharine's Dock; Alf, East Ham Jewish Cemetery; Peter Willasey, Harrods; John Lewis Partnership Archives; Stephen Green, Lord's; Barry Brown, PR Manager, Earl's Court and Olympia Ltd; Selfridges; Dereck Smith, London Canal Museum; Marks & Spencer; Wimbledon Lawn Tennis Museum.

Jason Hawkes:
I would like to thank Richard Atkinson for all his enthusiasm for this project, Olivia Wilson at Aerofilms and Ian Evans for his great help getting me up in the sky and providing the occasional sick bag.

First published in 2000 by
HarperCollins*Illustrated*,
an imprint of HarperCollins*Publishers*
77–85 Fulham Palace Road
London W6 8JB

The HarperCollins website address is
www.**fire**and**water**.com

Jason Hawkes' aerial photographic library can be contacted on
07071 226465 or at www.jasonhawkes.com

Aerofilms Limited are at Gate Studios, Station Road, Borehamwood, Herts WD6 1EJ;
tel 020 8207 0666; fax 020 8207 5433; email library@aerofilms.com

Contemporary photographs © 2000 Jason Hawkes
Archive photographs © 2000 Aerofilms Limited
Text © 2000 Ian Harrison

A CIP catalogue record for this book is available from the British Library

ISBN: 0 00 220215 8

04 03 02 01 00

9 8 7 6 5 4 3 2 1

Colour origination by Colourscan, Singapore

Printed and Bound by Printing Express Ltd., Hong Kong.